AF480977

BY - MICHAEL L. PINKARD JR.

Illustrated by:

AMERICAN WRITING SERVICES

DEDICATION

To my dear Grandfathers,

Jackson Graham, Bertrus Washington, Milton West, and Oliver Pinkard. Your unwavering attention, guidance, and boundless love have always been a source of inspiration for me, my sisters, and my cousins. This volume is also meant to pay homage to all of the grandparents out there who took time out to nurture, spoil, and sometimes raise their grandchildren far past what was expected of them. Thank you for your wisdom, encouragement, and the countless stories you've shared with us. This book is dedicated to you, the beacons of kindness and understanding whose presence has shaped my world in the most beautiful of ways.

I would also like to take this moment to thank my children's grandparents, Santiago & Lucy Robles. Thank you for all of the attention and love you have shown our children. You will forever be appreciated.

ACKNOWLEDGMENT

Michael. L. Pinkard Jr. was born and initially raised in North Omaha, Nebraska. From early on, his mother, renowned coach Wanda West, instilled in him the values of handwork, fair play, and sportsmanship. She discovered, when he was young, that he was gifted in sports, martial arts, and leadership. This gift he possessed resonated with his younger cousins that became more like siblings to him. My Big Cousin Mike stems from reflective stories narrated by Michael's younger cousin, Vernon Alexander West (AKA 'Vee'), referencing how Mike protected and positively influenced him and the other cousins.

Now he is a husband, father, teacher, coach, and a fundamental martial artist aiming to make a real impact through his experiences, philosophies, and education.

I was feeling nervous as today all my cousins and I were meeting at Grandpa Jack's house to prepare for the Annual Neighborhood 4th of July Water Balloon Competition. Grandpa Jack, a great man with a history of service, loved to coach us as we got ready to take on the other neighborhood families. He would get us the best water guns and spend the whole morning helping us fill water balloons while preparing for the neigh-borhood barbecue he enjoyed hosting after the contest was over.

02

My nerves were uneasy because our older and bigger cousin, Joseph, was staying at Grandpa's house. His parents were away, serving in the military. I'm unsure if it's because his parents were gone, but Joseph could be really mean sometimes. If he wasn't busy pushing us around, he was bragging about how much stronger and better he was at almost everything.

Boo!
04

When we arrived at Grandpa Jack's, I could see our younger cousins TJ, Danya, and baby Jennifer playing tag in the front yard through the car window. Grandpa Jack was probably cleaning the barbecue pit or using the water hose to fill the balloons in the backyard. It looked like they were having much fun, and I was almost excited to join them.

That was until I saw Joseph come from the side of the house, acting like some sort of monster. Our younger cousins' faces switched from joy to fear as they were pushed harshly onto the ground while trying to flee from him.

06

As Joseph stood there admiring his work, I got out of the car and started walking up the porch steps. With a teasing tone, Joseph said to me, "Hey Vernon, Mike isn't coming. He had better things to do. Do you want to play Jurassic Universe with us, or are you too chicken?" Jenny was getting off the ground, trying to hold back tears. Danya was dusting the dirt off her knees, and TJ, the youngest and most energetic among us, had already forgotten that Joseph knocked him down and was running around the yard with his hands in claw positions, roaring and yelling, "Dinosaur!"

RAWR!

"Let me go inside and say hi to Grandpa, then we will see," I replied. Just like I had imagined, I could see Grandpa Jack through the back door getting the grill ready when I went inside. His face lit up with joy when he saw me; he motioned me over for a hug. He said, "I bought some of those granola bars you like; go in the kitchen and grab one." I joyfully replied, "Yes sir!" Then, I hurried to the kitchen to get my granola bar.

On my way out, and because I was trying to open my treat, I didn't notice that Joseph had entered the house and was standing directly in front of me.

10

Joseph took my granola bar and pushed me to the ground. As I hit the floor, I heard someone yell, "Hey!" It was My Big Cousin Mike, who had just arrived at our grandpa's house. He noticed what was happening and stood up for me. He stood strong with the rest of my younger cousins behind him, looking like a team of superheroes coming to save the day.

Facing Joseph, Mike said, "This ends today! You will never be mean to us again, or you can find a new team for the water balloon competition and anything else we do together!"

13

14

It was obvious from the expression on his face that Joseph was surprised by their actions. His face went from startled to angry as he stared back at Mike. I didn't know what would happen! Suddenly, tears started streaming down Joseph's face as he said, "First, my parents left me, and then you started spending all your time with them! You never come over to play with me anymore!"

As I picked myself up off the floor, I realized why Joseph had been so mean. Not that it was okay, but I understood. Joseph was the only one of us who didn't have his parents and had to stay at Grandpa's house. Also, he and Mike used to play together all the time before the rest of us became old enough to join them. Grandpa Jack is the best, but Joseph had to be lonely over here with no one his own age to play with.

My Big Cousin Mike, seemingly without missing a beat, walked over to Joseph, gave him a hug, and said, "I'm sorry. I was wrong for leaving you alone here. Our job now is to protect and teach new things to our younger cousins, but I promise I will come to Grandpa's house more to see you." The rest of us joined the hug as Joseph apologized for being mean. We all promised Joseph that we would ask our parents to bring us over at least once a week to play with him. This seemed to make Joseph very happy.

3

Grandpa Jack returned inside and addressed us with great inspiration, saying, "Soldiers, are we ready to win this competition?" Grandpa Jack, a veteran we all admired, affectionately referred to us as "Soldiers". In unison, we replied, "Sir, yes sir!" "Good! Afterwards we're going to have the best barbecue this neighborhood ever tasted!" he exclaimed as we all picked up our water guns, grabbed the ice chest filled with water balloons, and headed outside to our base which was the front porch. The rules were simple: once your entire team was wet, you were out of the contest. Our strategy was to wet them all as soon as possible and keep our youngest one, TJ, completely dry.

20

Once we filled up all of our water guns, we asked TJ to protect our water balloons, which were still on the porch. He accepted the job with pride. Looking around the neighborhood, we saw all the other kids in front of their porches, ready for the event to begin. Every year, Grandpa Jack would yell "Begin!" to start the competition.

This year, he came outside wearing his Army uniform and took one look at us as we all stood together. He asked, "Is victory ours today?" Once again, we all shouted, "Sir, yes sir!" Then he loudly exclaimed, "Let the games begin!" After that, everyone headed out, and we had the best water gun and balloon engagement the world had ever seen. I won't say who won, but TJ never got wet!

After that day, Joseph occasionally said some not-so-nice things, but he never treated us poorly or hit us again. We all kept our promise, especially in the summer, and visited Joseph at Grandpa Jack's house at least once a week until his parents came back to pick him up. I was grateful that Mike was there to help us stand up for ourselves. I've said it before, and I'll say it again: I don't know what it was about him, but I was always happy when I knew my Big Cousin Mike was coming over.

THE END